CONTENTS

Introduction 4

Children's Games 6

Books and Reading 8

At the Theatre 10

Music 12

Rail Excursions 14

House Party 16

Lawn Tennis 18

Bank Holidays 20

Football 22

At the Wicket 24

Beside the Seaside 26

Staying in a Hotel 28

Glossary 30

Index 32

INTRODUCTION

Victorian working people had very little free time. They worked long hours and had few holidays, so any leisure time was a luxury. In the second half of the century, new laws shortened working hours and created bank holidays. This helped to make more spare and leisure time for the average working person. The expanding rail network also made travelling cheaper and easier, so that ordinary people could take day trips and even holidays to the new seaside **resorts**.

We use the word Victorian to describe the time when Queen Victoria was on the British throne. Born in 1819, Victoria was the only child of Edward, the fourth son of King George III, and Victoria Maria Louisa, the daughter of a German duke. She became queen in 1837, and three years later married Albert, a German prince. They had nine children before Albert died in 1861. Victoria ruled for almost 64 years, longer than any other British monarch. She died in 1901, at the age of 81.

Life in VICTORIAN Times

Sport & Leisure

Neil Morris

Belitha Press

First published in the UK in 1999 by
Belitha Press Limited, London House,
Great Eastern Wharf, Parkgate Road,
London SW11 4NQ

This edition first published in 2000

500 448364

ISBN 1 84138 149 7 (paperback)
ISBN 1 85561 890 7 (hardback)

British Library Cataloguing in Publication Data
for this book is available from the British Library.

Series editor: Honor Head
Series designer: Jamie Asher
Picture researcher: Diana Morris
Consultant: Sallie Purkis

Printed in Singapore

Picture credits

Words in **bold** are in the glossary on pages 30 and 31.

In the second half of the Victorian era many more people had the time and energy to play and watch various sports. Cricket had been played on village greens for centuries, and now it was organized into county and international matches. Rugby football was an **amateur** game played mainly by public schoolboys, and association football (or **soccer**) was taken up by working people as the national sport.

During the Victorian period music became popular with both rich and poor people. The wealthy went to concerts and held musical evenings at home, while poorer people enjoyed music halls. Playing music on the streets was even a way of making money.

Many people began to go to watch soccer on Saturday afternoons. By the end of the century, the football league and the FA Cup were well established and followed all over the country. Another national sporting institution was begun in 1877 with the first Wimbledon lawn tennis championships. By the end of the Victorian era, all these sports and others were much better organized for both players and spectators.

CHILDREN'S GAMES

Victorian children, both rich and poor, enjoyed playing games. The children of well-off parents were given their own toys to play with. Many had a wooden rocking horse in the nursery, and wooden building bricks. Most Victorian toys were handmade, though from the 1850s some toys were made in factories.

Poorer children played street games, such as hopscotch and leapfrog, which didn't cost anything. **Conkers** were free and marbles were cheap, so these became popular toys with poorer children. The streets were much safer than they are today, because there was so little traffic. In the country, the village **blacksmith** made cheap iron hoops that the children could play with.

Older children liked board games and playing cards. Before the days of radio or television, families would often spend an evening playing card games such as happy families, snap or beggar-my-neighbour. They played other games such as dominoes, backgammon and nine men's morris, as well as charades. In fact, many of the games that we might play at a party today come from Victorian times.

▶ *There were many different ways to play marbles. Most games were based on trying to roll your marbles as close to a target as possible.*

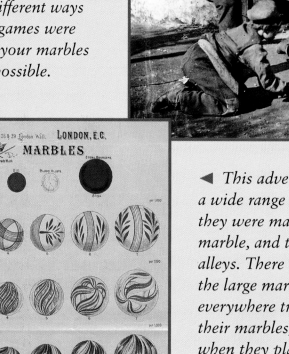

◀ *This advertisement from 1894 shows a wide range of marbles. Originally they were made of stone, especially marble, and the best were known as alleys. There were different sizes, and the large marbles were called taws. Boys everywhere treasured and looked after their marbles, hoping to win new ones when they played. Girls spent more time with their dolls or other games.*

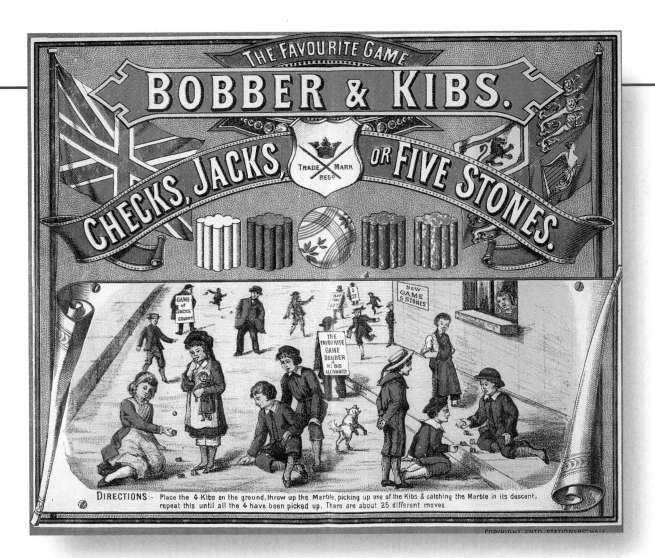

▲ Originally jacks was called knuckle-bones. It was played with five of the small bones that are found at the knuckle end of a leg of lamb. An 1890s book of games suggests: 'These bones are best for the purposes of the game if obtained after the meat has been cooked and cut away.' No wonder bought sets became popular!

► There were many different hoop games, and the most common was a straight race. In this 1897 advertisement the girl starter has a wooden hoop with a stick to knock it along. The boy racers have iron hoops and carry a special hook. This could be used to knock the hoop and guide it around corners.

BOOKS AND READING

Victorians were very keen to learn things, and many nineteenth-century authors wrote about how they thought people should behave. Among the most popular children's authors were the Grimm brothers, who collected and retold fairy tales such as *Hansel and Gretel*; Lewis Carroll, whose *Alice's Adventures in Wonderland* came out in 1865, and Anna Sewell, whose novel *Black Beauty* (1877) was a huge success. Charles Dickens was one of the most popular Victorian authors, along with the three Brontë sisters and George Eliot. The Brontës used male **pen-names**, and Eliot was a woman. Female writers pretended to be men so they would be taken more seriously.

When Elizabeth Gaskell wrote a book in 1853 about an unmarried mother, *Ruth*, local men burned copies and one even refused to let his wife read it. Lighter reading was considered more suitable for women, and cheap romantic books called novelettes were popular. Many magazines were published specially for female readers, such as *The Lady*, which is still published today.

▶ *Charles Dickens was born in 1812 into a poor family. At the age of 12 he was sent to work in a boot-polish factory. Many of his novels, such as* Oliver Twist *and* Little Nell, *describe the hardships of childhood and Victorian working-class life. Like many other popular novels at this time, his stories were* **serialized** *in weekly magazines. Readers had to wait for the next episode, just like today's television soap viewers. Dickens gave public readings of his novels to help sell them. This illustration shows his last performance, at St James's Hall, London, in 1870. He died three months later.*

Just after Victoria came to the throne, a Nottingham newsagent called Herbert Ingram moved to London to start a new weekly **periodical**. He was convinced that people would want to read a news magazine with lots of pictures. The Illustrated London News was first printed in 1842, and it was a huge success. This 1882 cover shows an attempt to shoot Queen Victoria as she left Windsor station. The attempt failed and the would-be **assassin** was arrested.

▲ Pictorial periodicals gave as much space to pictures as they did to words, just like many of today's newspapers. This double page from The Illustrated London News takes a light-hearted look at the university boat race to be rowed that Saturday in 1880. In fact, the race had to be postponed because of fog. Since Sunday was a day of rest the race was held on the following Monday. Oxford won by three lengths.

AT THE THEATRE

Victorians loved watching performances and entertainments of all sorts, and many theatres were built in towns and cities. In country villages, people watched plays and shows put on by travelling actors in their local hall. Before the days of electricity stages were lit by burning lime, which led to the phrase describing people as being 'in the limelight'.

The famous English actor Henry Irving made his first appearance at the Sunderland Theatre in 1856. He then acted in plays in Edinburgh, Manchester and Liverpool, before appearing at the St James's Theatre in London in 1866. Irving went on to become known as the greatest actor of his time for his appearances in Shakespeare's plays at the Lyceum Theatre. In 1878 he began a partnership with Ellen Terry, who became his leading lady for more than 20 years.

In 1881 the Savoy Theatre in London became the first in the world to be lit by electricity. It seated a thousand people and became the home for the **operettas**, or musical plays, of Gilbert and Sullivan.

◄ *This programme cover of 1898 shows prices ranging from one shilling (five pence) for a seat in the pit, or the back of the stalls. The London Pavilion opened as a music hall in 1861. Here all sorts of variety acts were performed, with singing, dancing and acting. A magician might also appear on the stage. Sometimes there were as many as 20 different performers and acts in one evening.*

▶ *Gilbert and Sullivan's* Pirates of Penzance *was first performed in London in 1879. The music was composed by Arthur Sullivan, and the words were written by William Gilbert. Gilbert and Sullivan wrote many operettas together and they were very popular with Victorian audiences.*

THE
PIRATES OF PENZANCE,

GALOP
CHARLES D'ALBERT.
LONDON. CHAPPELL & Co 50, NEW BOND ST W.

◀ *Theatres and halls were useful for all sorts of gatherings besides plays and variety acts. This music hall in Dublin sometimes held religious meetings.*

MUSIC HALL

◀ *Amateur **dramatics** were very popular. This photograph shows the cast of a play by Shakespeare,* The Merchant of Venice, *which was performed in Darjeeling, India, in 1891. The actors are British army officers who were serving in this part of the British Empire. Wives and daughters took the female roles.*

11

MUSIC

Playing and listening to music and singing were very popular pastimes for the Victorians. The **gramophone** was invented in America in 1887, but only came into general use in Britain later. Working-class people went to village halls, public houses or music halls to listen to music and join in a merry sing-song. Brass bands played popular tunes on bandstands in the parks. Many ordinary homes had an upright piano, and in the evening the whole family would gather around to sing their favourite songs. Instead of records and CDs, people bought **sheet music** and the words to the latest songs.

Better-off people held private concerts in their large houses and dressed up to go to concert halls in towns and cities. The Royal Albert Hall, in London, was named after Queen Victoria's husband and opened in 1871. This magnificent concert hall could hold more than 5000 people. The famous promenade concerts, at which the audience could stand or move about, were first held at the Queen's Hall in 1895. They continue at the Royal Albert Hall over 100 years later.

◀ *Young middle-class ladies were expected to have 'accomplishments' – certain social skills. These included being able to sing and play the piano. In wealthy families, daughters were trained to run their future homes and to entertain their guests. The skills they learned helped them to attract a suitable husband.*

▲ *Music appealed to people from all walks of life. This illustration shows some of the audience at a popular concert in St James's Hall, London, in 1872. At the time* St James's was London's leading concert hall. Great **composers** from all over the world, such as Dvorak, Grieg and Tchaikovsky, performed there.

◀ *Street musicians played a variety of instruments, such as the mouth organ and the barrel organ, to earn a living on the streets. The barrel organ looked rather like a small piano with a handle. When the handle was turned, a rotating cylinder inside hit a series of pipes, strings and metal tongues, making music. Some street musicians had dancing monkeys as an extra attraction.*

RAIL EXCURSIONS

Victorian working people had very little leisure time, and many had no extra money to spend on such luxuries as a holiday. But by the late 1840s the spread of the railways meant that some people could afford to go on day trips.

A stagecoach took about six hours to bump along the roads from London to Brighton. By 1860 Londoners could get to the sea in less than half that time by rail, and the fare was much cheaper. Some factories began organizing outings for their workers, or workers' groups and societies arranged them for themselves.

Thomas Cook (1808-92) organized his first railway trip in 1841, from Leicester to Loughborough. Ten years later he was offering cheap fares for working people to visit the Great Exhibition in London. By the end of the 1850s, Cook was organizing tours of wealthy British tourists to France, Switzerland and Italy. These were the beginnings of the modern **package holiday**.

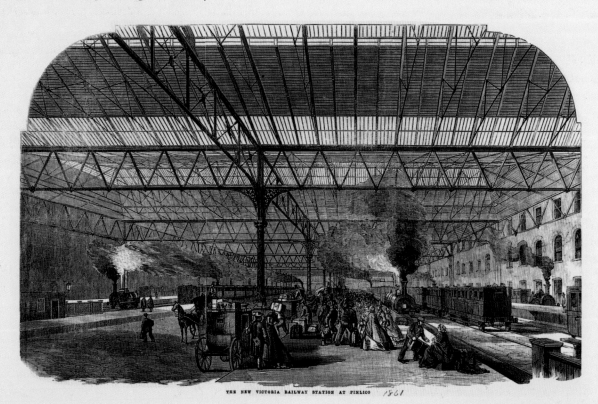

THE NEW VICTORIA RAILWAY STATION AT PIMLICO *1861*

▲ *Victoria Station, in London, opened on 1 October 1860, with 94 trains steaming in and out on its very first day. The new station had nine tracks and four platforms and served four railway companies: the London, Brighton and South Coast; the London and North Western; the London, Chatham and Dover; and the Great Western. There were separate booking rooms for the different classes, general waiting rooms and special ladies' rooms. Carriages took passengers directly to and from their train.*

THE ESTATE

▲ Margate, on the Kent coast, was popular with working-class day trippers from London. The trip made an ideal day out, as did a trip to Blackpool for the factory workers of Lancashire. Margate was already a popular coastal resort at the end of the eighteenth century, when a local man named Benjamin Beale invented the **bathing machine.** When the railways made day excursions cheap, the Margate beaches were soon full of Punch and Judy shows, donkey rides and people selling **whelks** and **eels.**

◄ An early South Eastern Railways train steams from Canterbury, in Kent, with the beautiful cathedral in the background. There were three different classes of railway carriage, which varied in comfort. Generally, rail excursions were becoming cheaper, easier and more comfortable.

HOUSE PARTY

Many rich families owned a large house in the country, surrounded by a big **estate**. They may also have had a **town house** in London or another big city. The owners of estates liked to hunt, shoot and fish in their spare time. Today many people are opposed to hunting as a sport, but in Victorian times it was considered great fun. Landowners invited their friends to join them in the hunt, and they had a big party at the house afterwards.

People were often invited to stay for the weekend. In the summer garden parties were very popular. The party-givers had very little work to do themselves, as they had servants to do it for them, from making the beds to doing the cooking and serving food and drinks. If the weather was good, the guests might play **croquet** on the huge lawn. In the evening they might listen to a piano recital given by one of the guests or the **hostess**. Sometimes the party-givers would hire a **quartet** to provide entertainment.

Towards the end of the Victorian period many of the very large country houses became too expensive for private families to keep up. Today, some of them belong to the National Trust, which was founded in 1895 to preserve places of historic interest. Today, we can all visit some of these stately homes.

◀ *This photograph shows a game of croquet being played in 1872. The house was in Croydon, just south of London, which was in the countryside at this time. A Victorian book of sports and pastimes said of croquet: 'It was the first successful attempt to invent an outdoor game in which both sexes could join on terms of equality.'*

◄ This invitation card showed that those lucky enough to receive it would have an enjoyable time at Sheerwater Court. Guests could play tennis, take tea under a shady tree in the garden and stroll to the neighbouring woodland.

► After-dinner games were very popular at house parties. This illustration shows a game of blind man's buff being played in 1874. The blindfolded player was turned around three times, then let go to try and catch someone else in the room. When he caught someone, he had to guess who it was. If he was right, that person was then blindfolded and the game continued.

◄ Many wealthy families had special house parties at Christmas, and guests would stay for the whole of the Christmas period. Part of the entertainment would include carol singing.

LAWN TENNIS

British army officer Major Walter Clopton Wingfield introduced a new game at a garden party in 1873. Major Wingfield called his game *sphairistike*, from the Greek for 'playing ball', saying that it was adapted from a game played by the ancient Greeks. The rules were based on the indoor game of real tennis, which originated in France. The game was played on a grass court shaped like an **hourglass** and divided by a high net. The new game quickly became very popular, changing its name to lawn tennis.

The Marylebone Cricket Club revised the Wingfield rules, and in 1877 the All England Croquet Club added Lawn Tennis to its title. The club held the first championship at its grounds in Wimbledon, south London. The only event in 1877 was the 'gentlemen's singles', contested by 22 players, and spectators paid one shilling (five pence) to watch the final. A ladies' singles event was added to Wimbledon in 1884, when doubles matches were also played.

Tennis was played for fun mainly by wealthy people. Players needed an expensive racket and tennis balls, and there were no public courts. Those who could afford it had a tennis court laid out on their lawn. Victorians were happy to allow men and women to play tennis together, just as they had croquet, and this increased its popularity.

*Tennis is at the centre of this presentation of sport and leisure outfits. Men wore long trousers and caps, and women wore long dresses and hats. The rackets were made of wood, with real **gut strings**. The game was much slower and less athletic than it is today.*

► *Victorian women enjoyed tennis. A book published in the 1890s stated: 'There is the special recommendation of lawn tennis that it can be played by girls as well as boys, and that ladies are not infrequently known to be able to hold their own in a double game, or even in a single game, against really excellent players belonging to the stronger sex.' Tennis clubs were mixed, unlike most other sports clubs.*

▼ *A scene from the 1891 Wimbledon men's singles final. In those days the defending champion went straight into the final, where he met the winner of that year's challenge tournament. In 1891 holder Joshua Pim played challenger Wilfred Baddeley and lost in four sets. Baddeley was 19 years old and remained the youngest men's champion until Boris Becker won in 1985. Baddeley defended the title successfully in 1892 and won again in 1895. Baddeley also won four doubles titles with his twin brother Herbert. The twins were so alike that opponents couldn't tell them apart.*

BANK HOLIDAYS

Early Victorians worked six days a week, with just Sunday off and two public holidays, Good Friday and Christmas Day. But gradually **employers** started to let their workers have Saturday afternoon off, too. Some even gave their **employees** an annual holiday, usually unpaid.

Then, in 1871, a new law allowed banks to close on four extra days – Easter Monday, **Whit Monday**, the first Monday in August and Boxing Day. Businesses found it difficult to trade when the banks were closed, so these days became public holidays, called bank holidays as they still are today. These became days when families did special things together, especially at Easter, Whitsun and Christmas.

The extra free time allowed people to keep up local traditions such as painting and hiding eggs at Easter, and parading through the street at Whitsun. In places such as Lancashire, children enjoyed egg-rolling at Easter. They rolled painted hard-boiled eggs down grassy slopes on Easter Monday. Sometimes they tried to hit each other's eggs just like a game of marbles.

▲ *On days out, picnics were very popular. Queen Victoria was apparently fond of picnics, and from the 1850s more people followed her example. This group have found themselves a shady spot in the park.*

*Picnic **hampers** were filled with food which was served on china plates. Meat pies, roast duck or pigeon were followed by jelly and fruit pudding, washed down with wine, beer and fruit squash.*

▼ Stanley Park, in Liverpool, was opened in May 1870 by the mayor of the city. Like many other city dwellers, Liverpudlians needed breathing space and room to walk and play on rest days and public holidays.

◀ Fairs travelled around the country, and were especially popular on bank holidays. This one was on Hampstead Heath, London, in 1900. Up to 100 000 people would go to the heath on a bank holiday if the weather was fine. Spring and summer fairs are still held there.

► In Victorian times every member of the household stirred the Christmas pudding for luck. They also put a sixpence or another coin in the pudding. The person who found it in their portion when it was served, could make a wish.

FOOTBALL

Victorians were very good at making and sticking to rules. In previous centuries, whole villages had challenged each other to rowdy games of football, but every village had its own special version of the game. Proper football rules were first written at Cambridge University in 1846. These were changed slightly when the Football Association was formed in 1863. The first FA Cup competition was held in 1872, when Wanderers beat Royal Engineers in the final in front of a crowd of 2000 at Kennington Oval.

According to sports legend, in 1823 a pupil at Rugby School named William Webb Ellis picked up the football during a match and ran with it. A new game was born – rugby football. Throughout Victorian times rugby union remained a strictly amateur game.

Association football, nicknamed soccer, quickly became professional and attracted large crowds every Saturday afternoon to watch the top clubs. By 1901, 110 000 people were watching the FA Cup Final at Crystal Palace. Soccer became the ordinary people's favourite game, to play and especially to watch.

▼ *A game of football at Rugby School in 1870. Although the ball was still round, they played to their own 'Rugby rules', which allowed handling and running with the ball. It appears that the touchlines were not very clearly marked and some spectators are in danger of becoming part of the game. Team members at Rugby were given caps. This led to other sports giving caps to international players, and this still happens today.*

PRESTON NORTH END

Well Played
"DRUMMOND"

▲ Preston North End Association Football Club was founded in 1881. Eight years later the club won the first ever football league championship, without losing a single match. In the same season, the Preston Invincibles, as they were known, won the FA Cup without giving away a single goal. G Drummond was one of the Preston heroes who went on to win the league title a second time in 1890.

◄ This picture shows two players having banged their heads together in the FA Cup Final of 1895, played between Aston Villa and West Bromwich Albion at Crystal Palace. Higgins of WBA (with his **shin guards** outside his socks) is falling down left, having clashed with Villa's Devey (right). Devey recovered to score the winning goal for Aston Villa. Later that year the FA Cup was stolen from a Birmingham shop window. Aston Villa were fined £25 to pay for a new cup for the 1896 competition.

► Victorian rugby players were more relaxed than rugby players today. There was very little training or coaching, and young men played for the fun of it.

AT THE WICKET

The game of cricket was played in England centuries before Victoria's time. In the early nineteenth century it was considered to be rather a rough game, played mainly on village greens. The rules were slightly different all over the country. But cricket was also played at the top **public schools**, such as Eton and Harrow, and old boys of these schools started forming clubs and playing for county teams.

Cricket became an important part of public school life, as many teachers thought that this and other team games were an important part of education. Learning to play according to the rules, to be a good sport and to accept defeat gracefully, built up a boy's character, they believed. Girls rarely played cricket, though some did take part in family games and the first women's club was founded in Yorkshire in 1887.

County matches were played throughout the century, and an official county championship was introduced in the 1890 season. By then internationals, called **test matches**, were also being played. The first was played in 1877 in Australia, and three years later the Australians played at the Oval cricket ground, in London.

▼ *This illustration shows a match at Lord's cricket ground in London in 1863. The match was between an All England XI and a United XI. Both teams were made up of great players of the time who toured the* counties to earn money and spread knowledge of the game. Lord's was the headquarters of world cricket and home of the Marylebone Cricket Club, or MCC, which controlled the laws of the game.

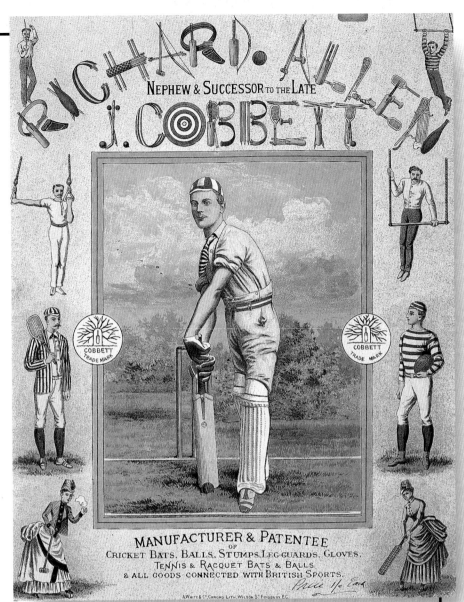

▲ Dr W G Grace (1848-1915), the captain of Gloucestershire, became known as the greatest cricketer in Victorian England and was a national hero. He played first-class cricket from the age of 16 until he was 60, scoring 54 896 runs as a batsman, including 126 centuries, and taking 2876 wickets as a bowler. Two of WG's brothers also played for Gloucestershire and England.

▲ This advertisement of 1887 shows how the serious Victorian batsman dressed. Rare batswomen (bottom right) were rather inhibited by their dress!

◄ These youngsters look well prepared for their game of cricket. The boy second from left has clearly been watching his elders leaning on their bat at the wicket. The boy next to him has a set of stumps.

BESIDE THE SEASIDE

The growth of railways meant more journeys to the coast for many people. Working people could only afford the time and money for day trips, but middle-class Victorians began to take a week's or fortnight's holiday at the seaside. During the 1860s seaside resorts grew very quickly. According to the national census of 1871, there were 56 such resorts, including Blackpool, Brighton, Hastings, Margate, Ramsgate, Scarborough and Torquay, with a total population of well over half a million.

Doctors recommended that people should go to the seaside for their health, as the air was so much cleaner than in the smoke-filled industrial cities. Bathing became popular for fun and exercise, though difficult because of the strict Victorian attitude towards any form of undress. Most bathing beaches were **segregated**, so that women would not be stared at.

As the seaside grew more and more popular, other entertainments sprang up. **Esplanades**, **piers** and **promenades** were popular with walkers. Funfairs, Punch and Judy shows, donkey rides, **pleasure gardens** and restaurants became regular attractions at seaside resorts.

▼ *Blackpool was one of the fastest growing resorts, mainly because it was easily reached by train from the industrial towns of Lancashire. This* **wrought-iron** *pier was opened in May 1863, watched by 20 000 visitors. It was 428 metres long and had shelters where people could sit and places that sold refreshments.*

▼ These ladies' bathing costumes of the 1880s were quite daring, because they showed bare arms and ankles. They must have been quite difficult to swim in, but people were less concerned about that. Women usually changed in bathing machines, which were towed into the sea by horses. Bathers could then get into the water without being seen. Men usually bathed naked, well away from the ladies' area.

▲ This poster boasts of the delights of Blackpool in 1889. By then there was a second pier, as well as other attractions. The resort has a 'high **sanitary** condition' and, happily, a 'low death-rate'. The famous sandy beaches were backed by 11 kilometres of built-up seafront, and in 1895 a 158-metre high tower was put up, modelled on the famous Eiffel Tower in Paris.

◄ The beach at Margate, Kent, in the 1890s. Some bathing machines have been towed out into the **shallows**, while others (costing sixpence) wait on the shore. People remained dressed while they were on the beach, and used hats and umbrellas to shade themselves from the sun.

STAYING IN A HOTEL

Visitors to the seaside and other holiday resorts often stayed in boarding houses, which were like small hotels. Many boarding houses were ordinary homes converted into places for paying guests and were run by the owner of the house, called the landlady. Guests usually had either bed and breakfast or full board, meaning accommodation and all meals.

Better-off people stayed in larger hotels. In late Victorian times, many hotels were built especially for this purpose and some of them still stand today. Standards improved as time passed, and owners put in many more bathrooms, lifts and telephones. Hotels such as the Savoy, in London, became famous all over the world. Hotels were generally expensive, but some rich people spent their time moving from one hotel to another.

Rich Victorians were great travellers. Railways and steamships encouraged them to travel abroad, especially in Europe, and the hotels of Paris, Rome and Vienna became popular with wealthy tourists. As the Victorian era drew to a close, the world was becoming a smaller place for many people.

▼ *A wet Sunday in a Welsh hotel in 1879. Guests try hard to amuse themselves by reading books and newspapers, playing the piano, studying photographs,* **crocheting**, *and simply dozing. There was little else to do on a Sunday since the billiards room would be shut and the smoking room would only open 'after* **chapel** *hours'.*

EASTBOURNE.

ALBION HOTEL

FOR FAMILIES AND GENTLEMEN.

TABLE D'HÔTE DAILY.

JAMES RUDD, Proprietor.

▼ London's Savoy Hotel opened in 1889, eight years after the neighbouring Savoy Theatre. Richard D'Oyly Carte (1844-1901) built the theatre to put on his Gilbert and Sullivan productions. Many London hotels were benefiting from all the visitors to his operettas, and he decided to offer this service himself. His hotel boasted the only electric lights and first 24-hour room service in the world. It was also the first London building to be made entirely of concrete and steel and not brick. It quickly became a favourite hotel of the rich and famous, and still stands today.

▲ This illustration of the Albion Hotel shows the beach and pier at Eastbourne in 1884. The hotel advertised itself for 'families and gentlemen' because it was very unusual for ladies to travel or stay anywhere on their own. The table d'hôte is a set meal at a fixed price.

Glossary

amateur a sport or activity followed for fun rather than money.

assassin a killer, especially someone who kills a political or other leader.

bathing machine a shed on wheels in which women could change at the seaside. The machine was pulled out into the sea by horses and back again after the person had finished swimming.

blacksmith a craftsman who worked with iron, especially shoeing horses.

chapel a place of worship.

composer a person who composes or writes music.

conker the hard fruit of a horse-chestnut tree.

crochet to make a piece of needlework by looping thread using a specially hooked needle.

croquet a game played on a lawn with balls that are hit through hoops with a mallet.

dramatics putting on and performing plays.

eel a fish, shaped like a snake, that people eat.

employee a person who works for someone for wages or pay.

employer a person who pays someone to do a job.

esplanade a long level area for walking beside the sea.

estate a large area of land, usually with a large house in the middle.

gramophone an old-fashioned record player with a turntable and needle.

gut string a strong cord made from the dried intestines of sheep and other animals and used as strings in some sports rackets and musical instruments.

hamper a large basket with a lid for carrying food, drink and crockery.

hostess a woman who entertains guests at her home (the male equivalent is a host).

hourglass a glass container that is pinched in the middle. It is full of sand which takes an hour to pass through the middle from the top to the bottom.

operetta a light opera or musical play.

package holiday a holiday with all the travel and hotel arrangements made in advance, for which holidaymakers are charged a single price.

pen-name a made-up name used by a writer to hide their identity. Emily Brontë's pen-name was Ellis Bell.

periodical a newspaper or magazine that comes out at regular intervals, usually monthly or weekly.

pier a long walkway built out to sea.

pleasure garden a garden that is especially laid out for visitors to enjoy looking at and walking through.

promenade a wide pavement along the seafront overlooking the beach.

public school a private school that charges fees. Children usually live there during termtime.

quartet a group of four musicians who play classical music.

resort a place where people take holidays.

sanitary describing conditions that affect people's health.

segregate to divide or keep separate. Segregated beaches had separate areas for men and women.

serialize to produce in a series of instalments, or parts.

shallows the area at the edge of the sea where the water is not very deep.

sheet music the printed words and musical notes of songs and other music published in separate sheets or booklets.

shin guards pads worn by footballers to protect their legs.

soccer a shorter word for association football

test match an international match, especially in cricket.

town house a house in town owned by someone who lives in the country.

whelk a type of shellfish that people eat.

Whit Monday the day after Whit Sunday, the seventh Sunday after Easter. The Whitsun weekend celebrates the descent of the Holy Spirit according to the Bible.

wrought iron a tough form of iron that can be shaped by beating and hammering or rolling.

Index

amateur dramatics 11

backgammon 6
bank holidays 4, 20
bathing 26
bathing costumes 7
bathing machines 15, 27, 31
Beale, Benjamin 15
Blackpool 26, 27
boarding houses 28
boat race 9
brass bands 12
Brontë sisters 8, 31

Canterbury 15
card games 6
Carroll, Lewis 8
charades 6
Christmas 17, 20, 21
concerts 12, 13, 16
conkers 6, 31
Cook, Thomas 14
cricket 5, 18, 24, 25
croquet 16
Crystal Palace 22, 23

Dickens, Charles 8
dominoes 6

Eastbourne 29
Easter 20
electricity 10, 28
Ellis, William Webb 22
excursions 14, 15

FA cup 5, 22, 23
fairs 21
football 4, 22
football league 4, 23

games 6, 7, 17
garden parties 16
Gaskell, Elizabeth 8
Gilbert and Sullivan 10, 11, 29
Grace, WG 25
gramophone 12
Great Exhibition 14
Grimm Brothers 8

Hampstead Heath 21
holidays 4, 14, 15, 20, 21, 26
hoops 6, 7
hopscotch 6
hotels 28, 29
hunting 16

Illustrated London News 9
Irving, Henry 10

jacks 7

leapfrog 6
limelight 10

magazines 8
marbles 6
Margate 27
Marylebone Cricket Club 18, 24
musicals 10, 11
music halls 5, 10, 11, 12

National Trust 16
nine men's morris 6

operettas 10, 11

parks 21
piano 12, 16
picnics 20
playing cards 6
public schools 24
Punch and Judy 15

quartet 16
Queen Victoria 4, 9

Royal Albert Hall 12
Rugby football 5, 22
Rugby school 22

seaside 4, 14, 15, 26
Sewell, Anna 8
Shakespeare 10, 11
soccer 5, 9
street musicians 13

tennis (see Wimbledon) 5, 18, 19
Terry, Ellen 10
test matches (cricket) 24
theatre 10

Victoria station 14

Wimbledon Tennis Championships 5, 18, 19